PRACTICE TESTS FOR CAE

TEACHER'S BOOK

Susan Morris
and
Alan Stanton

Longman Group Limited,
Edinburgh Gate
Harlow
Essex
CM20 2JE, England
and Associated Companies throughout the world.

© Susan Morris and Alan Stanton 1994
First published by Thomas Nelson and Sons Ltd 1994

This impression Longman Group Ltd 1996
ISBN 0-175-56296-2

All rights reserved; no part of this publication may be reproduced, stored in a retrieval system, or transmitted in any form or by any means, electronic, mechanical, photocopying, recording, or otherwise without either the prior written permission of the Publishers or a licence permitting restricted copying in the United Kingdom issued by the Copyright Licensing Agency Ltd.,
90 Tottenham Court Road, London W1P 9HE

Produced through Longman Malaysia, PP

Acknowledgements
UCLES for sample answer sheets (pages 66-68).

Contents

INTRODUCTION 4
Question Formats, Marking & Grading, Advice to Students
Paper 1: Reading 5
Paper 2: Writing 7
Paper 3: English in Use 9
Paper 4: Listening 12
Paper 5: Speaking 14

Answer Key and Tapescripts

Test 1
Paper 1: Reading 17
Paper 2: Writing 17
Paper 3: English in Use 18
Paper 4: Listening 19
Paper 5: Speaking 25

Test 2
Paper 1: Reading 28
Paper 2: Writing 28
Paper 3: English in Use 29
Paper 4: Listening 30
Paper 5: Speaking 37

Test 3
Paper 1: Reading 39
Paper 2: Writing 39
Paper 3: English in Use 40
Paper 4: Listening 41
Paper 5: Speaking 47

Test 4
Paper 1: Reading 49
Paper 2: Writing 49
Paper 3: English in Use 50
Paper 4: Listening 51
Paper 5: Speaking 55

Test 5
Paper 1: Reading 57
Paper 2: Writing 57
Paper 3: English in Use 58
Paper 4: Listening 59
Paper 5: Speaking 64

Introduction

The **Certificate in Advanced English** is a post-First Certificate exam which was launched by UCLES in 1991 and is offered twice a year, in June and December. There are five papers:

PAPER 1 READING 1 hour with 15 minutes additional transfer time to record answers on the answer sheet

PAPER 2 WRITING 2 hours

PAPER 3 ENGLISH IN USE 1 hour 30 minutes

PAPER 4 LISTENING approximately 45 minutes

PAPER 5 SPEAKING approximately 15 minutes

All five papers receive equal weighting of 20 per cent.

The examination questions are task-based and simulate real-life tasks that candidates might encounter, if they are using English in work situations, for example. The difficulty of the exam should not be underestimated. Candidates need to be able to process long texts fairly quickly. Paper One has a total word count of about 3,000 words. All the questions are text-based. This means that there is always something to read before the task can be done. Even the Writing Paper involves a considerable amount of reading. The lexical level is much closer to CPE than to FCE. Candidates must have good reading skills, and have become familiar with a wide range of texts, in order to do well in this exam.

Rubrics in CAE tend to be longer than in FCE and CPE and need to be read with great care since they play an important role in providing contexts for the questions. Correct spelling is important in all papers.

INTRODUCTION

PAPER 1 READING

WHAT DOES THE PAPER CONSIST OF?

Paper 1 Reading consists of four authentic texts (from, for example, newspapers and general interest magazines) amounting to some 3000 words in total. A text may be one continuous piece of writing, or may be made up of a number of smaller pieces. Understanding of the text is tested in a variety of ways: by *matching exercises*, where the candidate has to match information in the text to the person or thing it refers to, or to select suitable headings for sections of the text from a list provided; *gapping,* where sections of text have been removed from the main body of the text and are printed separately, so that the candidate has to determine which extract from the text should appear in which position; and *multiple-choice*, where the candidate has to choose the correct answer, A, B, C or D. There are between 40 and 50 questions to be answered on each paper.

Candidates need to be able to use a number of reading techniques in order to handle this length of text within the required time. They must have been trained how to scan the text for specific information, skim to form an overall impression of the gist of a text, select relevant information required to perform a task, interpret attitude, style and inference on the part of the writer, demonstrate awareness of the structure of a text and deduce meaning from context.

HOW IS THE PAPER MARKED?

Paper 1 is objectively marked by an Optical Mark Reader (OMR), a computer system which is able to detect marks on paper. Candidates transfer their answers to the reading questions onto an answer sheet using pencil, and this sheet is then read by the OMR.

WHAT ADVICE SHOULD I GIVE STUDENTS?

PART 1: Before the exam

- Read as much English as possible.
- Read a wide variety of different types of text.
- Develop an awareness of the different types of reading strategy needed in particular situations.

INTRODUCTION

- Practise skimming texts and summarising briefly what the content is.
- Practise scanning texts to find the answer to particular questions, ignoring the rest.
- Become conscious of how texts are structured by increasing awareness of the role of cohesive devices, such as linking words.

PART 2: In the exam

- Concentrate on the task set rather than worrying about unfamiliar words.
- Read the questions before reading the text.
- Work at a reasonable speed, not too fast but not wasting time.
- Realise that sometimes skimming and scanning are necessary, but at other times reading for detail is necessary. Develop an awareness of what strategy is required when.
- In multiple-matching tasks, take one of the people (or places etc.) from the text, (A, for example) and match against the points. Do this for all the people, places and so on in turn. Any points left must refer to the last person or place on the list.
- When choosing headings, remember that important information is often contained in the first and last sentences of each paragraph, so pay special attention to these.
- In the gapped text exercise, look carefully at the sentence that comes before and the one that comes after the gap, and make sure the extract you choose fits both. When you have completed all the gaps, always read through the complete text to check that it reads well as a whole.
- Transfer answers to the answer sheet in the fifteen minutes allowed at the end of the exam (an example of the answer sheet for this paper is on p. 66).
- Mark answers in pencil.
- Check carefully that the answers are transferred correctly to the answer sheet, and that the correct lozenges have been completed.

PAPER 2 WRITING

WHAT DOES THE PAPER CONSIST OF?

Paper 2 Writing consists of two sections, Section A, which is compulsory, and Section B, where the candidate does one writing task from a choice of four. Each of the two questions is marked out of the same total. In Section A, the candidate is required to write one or more pieces in response to a large reading input, and has to write a total of approximately 250 words. The same word total applies to the question chosen in Section B.

Paper 2 in CAE is called 'Writing', and the fact that this word is used rather than 'Composition' should alert candidates to the fact that there is in this paper an emphasis on the demonstration of writing skills for practical purposes. Each question makes it explicit to the candidate what the purpose of the writing task is and who the potential reader will be. There are clear indications of the required content.

This paper requires the candidate to be able to produce a variety of writing formats, not all of which will occur in any one paper. Candidates must be aware of the appropriate layout and style of: letters (both personal and business), reports, notes, instructions, messages, announcements, articles, brochures, advertising material. They must write in the appropriate form, using suitable layout and register.

HOW IS THE PAPER MARKED?

Each question is marked on a six-point scale from 0 to 5. There is a general impression mark-scheme that applies to all questions and refers to general features, such as:

- the effect on the target reader
- natural and accurate use of language
- use of a range of vocabulary and grammatical structures
- choice of relevant material to complete the task, with no omissions
- use of an appropriate register to complete the task
- use of a variety of cohesive devices
- clear and consistent organisation of material

There is also a task specific mark-scheme produced for each particular question outlining the content required. Each paper is marked independently by two trained examiners, and the scores are added together to provide the total mark for this paper.

INTRODUCTION

WHAT ADVICE SHOULD I GIVE STUDENTS?

- First read each question very carefully at least twice.
- Identify the important words in the instructions.
- Mark key words in the instructions, and come back to these at different stages in your planning to check you are taking them into account.
- Pay particular attention to any specific content words.
- Think carefully about who you are writing to and why. The roles of different people and your relationship with them is a key factor in how you write to them and how the examiners assess your writing. Adapt what you say to the person you are writing to.
- Consider exactly what you are being asked to write (a letter, a report, an article etc.) and use the appropriate format and register.
- Organisation and layout must be given attention at the planning stage, and not as an afterthought.
- You are unlikely in the exam to have sufficient time to write a first draft and then copy it out. Instead, make a plan of what you intend to write, using brief notes as a guide.
- Check that your grammar and spelling are correct.
- Use a range of vocabulary and grammatical structures.
- Remember that paragraphing is important in certain kinds of writing, such as letters, and plan it. Remember that it will be too late to incorporate paragraphs once the piece is written.
- Effective writing produces a favourable response in the target reader, and brings together appropriate content, format and language. Think about these three factors at the planning stage.
- Write your answer in ink.
- Checking what you have written is an important part of the writing process, so when you have finished a piece of writing *always* check it carefully.

INTRODUCTION

PAPER 3 ENGLISH IN USE

WHAT DOES THE PAPER CONSIST OF?

Paper 3 English in Use, consists of three sections (A, B and C) with two texts in each section. There are approximately 75 questions on the six texts. The paper lasts one and a half hours, including the time needed to complete the answer sheet.

Section A consists of two gap-fill texts. Text 1 has fifteen gaps. Candidates must choose the correct word for each gap from a choice of four words which appear on the paper. These words are **not** structural words such as 'was', 'have' and 'the'. They are lexical items which are similar in meaning such as 'brave', 'courageous', 'bold' and 'intrepid', only one of which is correct in the context of the text. For this question candidates write the correct letter (A,B,C or D) against each question number of the answer sheet.

Text 2 has fifteen gaps. The missing words are all structural words, none of which are given on the paper. For this question, candidates write one appropriate word against each question number on the answer sheet.

In **Section B**, text 3 contains errors of various kinds that have to be identified or corrected. Some texts have additional unnecessary and incorrect words and/or words missing. Other texts have spelling or punctuation errors. Between two and five lines of the text have no errors. When errors occur, there is one per line. For this question candidates write the unnecessary or missing word on the answer sheet, or the correct spelling or punctuation. Correct lines must be indicated by writing a tick (✔) on the answer sheet.

Text 4 is in two parts. The first part is a complete text but the second part, which is on the same topic as the first, has fifteen gaps which can be filled with one or two words. The information needed to complete the gaps can be found in the first part, but the actual words do not appear there. There is a difference in register between the two parts: for example, a formal letter followed by an informal note conveying the same information to a different person. For this question candidates write one or two words against each question number on the answer sheet.

In **Section C**, text 5 contains gaps which can be completed by selecting from ten phrases and clauses listed below the text. Some of these phrases/clauses do not fit at all. Candidates write one letter (A-I) against each question number on the answer sheet.

Text 6 consists of brief notes on a topic. Each set of notes has to be expanded into one complete sentence. Candidates write their sentences in the numbered spaces on the answer sheet.

INTRODUCTION

HOW IS THE PAPER MARKED?

Paper 3 is marked by trained markers using a mark-scheme. An examiner is present during the marking and may modify the mark-scheme if it is appropriate to do so.

Candidates' answers to the questions on texts 2, 4 and 6 which are fairly open-ended, are likely to show additional acceptable answers. In the light of this, the examiner may add these correct answers to the original mark-scheme. Each sentence in the answer to text 6 receives a mark of 0, 1 or 2. After they have been marked, the answer sheets can be read by an optical mark reader. Although candidates are permitted to write on the question paper, it is vital that all answers are transferred to the answer sheet.

WHAT ADVICE SHOULD I GIVE STUDENTS?

For all questions, study the example answers carefully. These will show the kind of answer that is required. If you do the questions out of sequence, be very careful that you write your answers in the correct order on the answer sheet.

Section A

- For *text 1* read through the whole text quickly to get an overall impression.
- Consider which of the four words seem to be wrong and why. The word you then choose as the correct answer may be one that you do not know.
- For *text 2* read through the whole text quickly to get an overall impression.
- Remember that the missing words are very short words such as 'than', 'to' and 'so'. Look at the grammatical context for clues both in the sentence where the gap is and throughout the passage. Identifying passive forms of verbs or comparatives may help you to decide which word is missing.
- Guess if necessary. No answer means no mark but you do not lose marks by giving a wrong answer.

Section B

- For *text 3* read the rubric carefully and see what kind of error(s) you have to look for.
- Look out for unnecessary prepositions after verbs and for words such as 'that', 'any', 'it' and 'been' which are not needed.
- Remember that most lines will have an error.
- For *text 4*, identify the change in register. Is the first part more formal, or more informal, than the second part?

- Remember that the first part contains all the information that you need but not the words.
- Read the rubric to find out the maximum number of words that you can write in in a gap. If the maximum is two, you can use one or two words in each gap.

Section C

- For *text 5* look carefully at words such as 'it', 'they' 'which', 'therefore' and 'so' and try to work out what they refer to. This will help you to follow the sequence of ideas.
- Consider whether the writer is giving an example, making an additional point, pointing out a disadvantage, etc. This will help you to choose an appropriate answer.
- Guess if necessary.
- For *text 6* write one sentence for each set of points. Do not write two short sentences.
- You can add words but do not add information.
- Make sure you understand the common abbreviations (e.g. DOB, 20th c.) that may occur in the notes.
- Try and join clauses with connectives such as 'which', 'whose' and 'although' etc., as well as simple linking words such as 'and'.
- You can change the form of words in the notes, from noun to adjective, for example.
- There is room on the question paper to make a first draft of your answer but make sure that your sentences are transferred to the answer sheet.

INTRODUCTION

PAPER 4 LISTENING

WHAT DOES THE PAPER CONSIST OF?

Paper 4 Listening, consists of four sections, Section A, B, C and D. Sections A, C and D are played twice, but Section B is played only once.

Sections A and B are informational pieces that are monologues. Section C has two or more speakers and in this as well as the other sections, there may be a variety of accents in the English spoken. Section D consists of brief snippets of English, and candidates have to recognise the role and attitude of the speakers.

HOW IS THE PAPER MARKED?

Candidates transfer their answers to the answer sheet which is then marked by an optical mark reader.

WHAT ADVICE SHOULD I GIVE STUDENTS?

PART 1: Before the exam

- Use every opportunity to listen to English.
- Listen to English in as many different situations as possible, e.g. conversation, radio, TV, films, videos, lectures, talks.
- Get used to the different ways people speak English.
- Listen to different accents.
- The more English you listen to, the less anxiety you will feel about listening in the exam.
- When listening to different speakers, think about how they indicate their role and attitude.
- Learn to listen not just to what people say but the way they say it.
- Become familiar with the formats of different questions in the exam, and practise working with these.

INTRODUCTION

PART 2: In the exam

- Don't allow yourself to get too anxious – although candidates often feel the listening paper is the most difficult, this isn't so. Most candidates do well in this paper.
- Answer each question as required: if a letter (e.g. A, B, C etc.) is needed, use this, not a lengthy paraphrase that might lead to mistakes; if a few words are needed, don't write a long answer.
- Concentrate on the keywords of an answer.
- If numbers are needed in the answer, then write numbers and not words – this avoids the danger of spelling mistakes.
- Take care in transferring answers to the answer sheet.
- Check this transfer to ensure that no mistakes have been made in the transfer procedure, particularly that:
  - you have put the right answer for the appropriate question
  - you have not written singulars where you meant to use plurals and vice-versa
  - you have not left out important words
  - your spelling is correct.

INTRODUCTION

PAPER 5 SPEAKING

WHAT DOES THE PAPER CONSIST OF?

This is the oral part of the examination. Candidates are examined in pairs and there are two examiners, the interlocutor and the assessor. Both examiners talk to the candidates and award marks but the interlocutor talks more and the assessor concentrates on awarding the correct mark to each candidate. This part of the examination lasts about fifteen minutes. It is possible to have three candidates and two examiners, in which case the interview lasts 23 minutes.

There are four phases:

Phase A consists of everyday social language. The examiners introduce themselves and the candidates talk about each other or find out about each other depending on whether they know each other or not. This phase lasts about three minutes.

Phase B is an information gap exercise. One candidate is given a picture and asked to describe it in such a way that the other candidate can say how it is similar or different from a picture that he or she has. Then the candidates change roles, using a different set of pictures. Each candidate is able to speak for about a minute, with occasional questions or comments from the other candidate. This phase lasts three or four minutes.

Phase C is a problem solving task, using a picture as a stimulus. The interlocutor will explain exactly what the problem is but does not take part in the discussion. The candidates talk to each other and may or may not reach agreement on the solution. This phase lasts about three or four minutes.

In **Phase D** the interlocutor and the assessor will join in the discussion at this point and both examiners and both candidates discuss the points raised in Phase C. This phase lasts three or four minutes.

When the candidates have left the room, the examiners discuss their marks and reach agreement on the marks for each candidate.

HOW IS THE PAPER MARKED?

Examiners mark according to five criteria:

Fluency

This refers to natural speed and rhythm without excessive hesitation. Normal pauses for thought and re-phrasing are acceptable.

INTRODUCTION

Accuracy and range

This refers to the variety, quality and accuracy of the grammatical structures and vocabulary used.

Pronunciation

This refers to individual sounds and features of connected speech such as word stress, sentence stress and intonation. Candidates achieving the highest marks may exhibit features of L1 accent but this will not inhibit communication.

Task achievement

This refers to the manner in which the candidate has carried out the tasks in the four phases and covers the following:
- fullness of contributions to the task/discussion
- appropriate use of vocabulary
- coherence and relevance of contributions
- independence in carrying out tasks (i.e. the degree to which candidates can carry out tasks without prompting or redirection by the interlocutor or the other candidate)
- the organisation of contributions
- flexibility and resourcefulness in explaining things

Interactive communication

This refers to the ability to take turns and participate actively in discussions with one, two or three others. Marks are given on a scale of 0–8. Candidates are given marks as individuals, not as a pair.

WHAT ADVICE SHOULD I GIVE STUDENTS?

Do not say that you 'don't know' about a particular topic. The point of the interview is for you to speak, so you must find something relevant to say.

Do not panic if you are given a picture and realise that you do not know the words to describe what is in it. Use circumlocutory expressions such as 'the thing in the corner' and 'the stuff he's carrying'. If you do not know the word 'hands' in relation to clocks, you can say 'the things that point to the numbers'.

There are advantages in being in a pair with someone you know because you should feel more relaxed. Do not try to rehearse what you will say because this will be obvious to the examiners and they may interrupt you with questions that require unrehearsed answers.

INTRODUCTION

There are also advantages in being in a pair with someone you don't know because you can ask genuine information-seeking questions which will make the interview seem very realistic.

Do not worry if you think that your partner is much better or worse than you. You may be wrong about this and, in any case, the examiners are not comparing you with your partner. They are giving you each a separate mark according to the assessment criteria. Remember that in Phase B you have a 'long turn' when you can speak at length.

Co-operate with your partner, take turns, ask questions and provide opportunities for your partner to continue speaking on the same topic by asking questions or making statements which invite a response. You will both do better if you co-operate with each other.

If you do not understand something that your partner or the interlocutor has said, ask for clarification. Carrying out the task depends on understanding what the interlocutor has asked you to do. If you are not sure if you have understood something, ask for further explanation. Do not attempt to continue if you are at all uncertain.

In Phases B and C, talk to your partner, not the interlocutor.

When entering and leaving the room, use the normal social greetings appropriate to the time of day.

Test 1

ANSWER KEY

PAPER 1 READING

FIRST TEXT

1 B 2 C 3 A 4 B 5 A 6 A 7 B 8 B 9 D 10 C 11 D 12 C 13 B 14 C 15 D 16 C 17 C 18 D

SECOND TEXT

19 C 20 B 21 D 22 D 23 B 24 B

THIRD TEXT

25 D 26 A 27 F 28 E 29 B

FOURTH TEXT

30 H 31 A 32 D 33 F 34 C 35 C 36 D 37 C 38 B 39 C 40 C 41 D

PAPER 2 WRITING

Notes for guidance

The writing tasks can be answered in a number of different ways but in every case the tone must be appropriate to the target audience and the subject matter and all the points in the questions must be covered in the answers. Here, as in the answer key for Tests 2–5, comments on each question can be given to students as advice before they start writing, or used as points to look for when marking students' work.

SECTION A

1a The letter must be polite but firm. Begin 'Dear Mr Wolff' and end 'Yours sincerely' followed by your signature and printed name. When writing letters in English, if you know the person's name use it. Important points are:

- the clause in the contract should not apply in this case – use information in the newspaper article to argue this point

TEST 1

– the £30 offered is not the equivalent of $100 – refer to the exchange rates.

b The postcard should be friendly, light-hearted and fairly simple – it is being sent to a six year old boy who may have only just learned to read. Do not refer to the problems with the insurance company. Enquire in general terms about Larry's health and perhaps express a wish to return to Florida in the future. Postcards do not begin with 'Dear –'.

SECTION B

2 Since this is a newspaper article, it should have a headline and possibly subheadings. The article must refer to *two* or *three* restaurants. For each restaurant, a particular (and different) aspect must be emphasised. There is no need to cover every aspect of each restaurant. Newspaper articles about restaurants normally end with the name, address and telephone number of the restaurant and its opening hours.

3 Remember that your friend is staying for one year and consider how this affects the advice you give. Refer to paying bills, getting things repaired etc. The letter could include a list of instructions. It is an informal piece of writing and should include contracted forms, e.g. It's, I'd.

4 This is a letter of application not a curriculum vitae. It must be written in sentences, not in note form. Begin 'Dear Sir or Madam' and end 'Yours faithfully'. At the beginning of the letter say which post you are applying for and which newspaper you saw the advertisement in, e.g., 'I am writing to apply for the post of Administrative Assistant for the Melchester Arts Festival, as advertised in 'The Times' on 11 April.' Include personal details (age, marital status), qualifications and experience. Show how your past experience relates to the requirements of the job. Mention the names, addresses and telephone numbers of two referees and say what position they hold. At the end of the letter, say when you are available to be interviewed.

5 As this is a magazine article, it should have a headline. The article may include lists of points. You must cover four things – pleasures, problems, equipment and costs. Remember that you are writing for readers who know nothing about the sport or hobby you have chosen.

PAPER 3 ENGLISH IN USE

SECTION A

1   **1** D **2** B **3** B **4** D **5** A **6** A **7** A **8** C **9** D **10** D **11** A **12** A **13** A **14** B **15** B

2   **16** within **17** there **18** much/strong **19** all **20** ever **21** what **22** even **23** though **24** a **25** did **26** longer **27** this **28** least **29** will **30** as

TEST 1

SECTION B

3   **31** up   **32** the   **33** human   **34** such   **35** ✔   **36** with   **37** unique   **38** ✔   **39** sharp   **40** of   **41** themselves   **42** ✔   **43** have   **44** ✔   **45** some

4   **46** attended   **47** at 2 p.m. (or similar time)   **48** dissatisfaction   **49** samples/products   **50** agreement   **51** effective   **52** point/complaint   **53** to contact   **54** evening   **55** deserted/closed/empty   **56** contacted them/told them   **57** informed   **58** ignorant/unaware   **59** to investigate   **60** a future/a later/the next

SECTION C

5   **61** C   **62** B   **63** A   **64** F   **65** G

6   (Model answers)

66 It is within easy reach of London and only 35 kilometres from the coast of France, which can be seen on a clear day.

67 Every year it is used by thousands of motorists who take ferries to and from France and there is also a lot of commercial traffic.

68 Many people pass through Dover very quickly but there is much to see and it is worth staying a few days.

69 There are many famous sights, including the White Cliffs, Dover Castle, which dates from 1160, the Roman lighthouse and some interesting museums.

70 On the Promenade is a statue of Matthew Webb, who in 1875 became the first man to swim from Dover to Calais.

71 In 1909 Louis Bleriot became the first man to cross the Channel in an aeroplane and the place where he landed, near the castle, is marked by a memorial in the shape of an aeroplane.

72 For more information about Dover, visit the Tourist Information Office in Townwell Street or phone 0304 205108.

PAPER 4 LISTENING

SECTION A

1 A753   **2** Art in Italy   **3** handout   **4** mail/post

5 TMA's (tutor-marked assignments)/how to study for the course

6 how to study for the course/TMA's (tutor-marked assignments)

7 4   **8** late   **9** guide   **10** typed   **11** (written) report

12 a bibliography/a list of books used

TEST 1

SECTION B

13 6.55 **14** derailment **15** goods **16** to (or from) Wales **17** no/none **18** X **19** ✓ **20** ✓ **21** ✓

SECTION C

22 younger **23** the Actor's Union
24 television ⎤
25 radio   ⎬ (in any order)
26 theatre   ⎦
27 type of role ⎤
28 earnings/pay ⎦ (in any order)
29 in their forties **30** experience **31** writers **32** women
33 monitoring roles   ⎤
34 avoiding sex stereotyping ⎦ (in any order)

SECTION D

Task one
35 B **36** D **37** G **38** F **39** A

Task two
40 J **41** K **42** L **43** I **44** O

TAPESCRIPT

SECTION A

You will hear a lecturer talking to students at the beginning of their course. Listen to the recording and fill in the information for questions 1–12 with a few words. You do not need to write full sentences. You will hear the recording twice.

Well, good morning everyone. My first task this morning, and it's a very happy one for me to perform, is to welcome all of you to this first tutorial for the University of Brancaster course A753 on Art in Italy. I'll be passing around a paper on which I'd like you to write your names, so that I know exactly who's been present, and, as is the case for all tutorials, this also means that if anyone who should be here is not, then I'll be able to put any of the handouts given out during the tutorial in the post, so that you'll get the essential information in some form or other, if not necessarily from the horse's mouth. Now there are two basic areas that I intend to deal with today. Past experience has shown that students starting the course have two areas of anxiety: the first is with how their work is going to be assessed, and the second is how best to study for the course.

As you will know if you've read the information sent to course participants before the start of the course, you will be required to supply four pieces of written work for assessment purposes. Each of these Tutor Marked Assignments or TMA's as we call them must be submitted by the date laid down in your course details, and it is absolutely necessary to meet this requirement. No late assignments will be marked, whatever the reason, whatever the reason for their being late, and your grade for the course will be affected.

Now I have some more important remarks to make about the actual mechanics of TMA writing. Although, as I have said, it is essential that you submit your assignment by the required date, I don't want you to feel too worried when you sit down to write the first one. Regard it as a chance to learn from the mistakes you're bound to make.

Word length is always laid down, and for the first TMA it is two thousand words. You can regard this as a guide, and anything within five hundred words either way will be acceptable. Remember that it is important to consider the question carefully and address yourself to the relevant issues. Length isn't an automatic indicator of quality. Legibility is important, it always helps if what you've written is easy to read. For this reason, we always prefer assignments to be typed if at all possible. If this is not possible, then please write as clearly as you can, allowing good margins so that comments can be written in. And it will help if you write on one side of the paper only. You'll also be receiving a separately written report on what you've submitted, with a grade.

At the end of your assignment, be sure to include all your sources of information – a bibliography including information about publisher and date should appear at the end of the assignment, and don't forget to acknowledge quotations. Now before I move on to talk about how best to study for the course, would anyone like to ask any questions?

SECTION B

You will hear a radio announcement about travel problems on the railway. For questions 13–17 make notes to complete the information. For questions 18–21 put a tick or a cross in the box as appropriate. Listen very carefully because you will hear this piece only once.

More now about that derailment earlier this morning on the main line from Wales to London Paddington. This is causing train passengers into London from the west severe disruption. Just before 7 am this morning, at 6.55, a goods train left the track just to the west of Swindon, blocking the main line from Wales. Luckily, latest reports from police and ambulancemen who reached the scene indicate that no one has been injured, and of course there were no passengers on the train, but the derailment has blocked the track, and it will be some hours before the line can be cleared.

This means that all trains from South Wales, that is from Swansea, Cardiff and Newport, will be subject to heavy delay. These trains, and I repeat, that is those trains from Swansea, Cardiff and Newport, will be routed through Bristol and Bath.

Trains from the West Country passing through Swindon are not affected, according to the latest information we have received, neither are trains from Gloucester to Swindon. Passengers travelling from Bristol Temple Meads, Bath and Chippenham to London Paddington should therefore experience no delay. However, trains travelling *from* London Paddington, to all destinations, are likely to suffer some disruption. We understand that trains *to* Wales will be re-routed via the northward route through Gloucester, which will result in considerably increased journey times.

So, not a good day for commuters into London from the west this morning, and a poor outlook for those travelling out of Paddington.

SECTION C

You will hear a radio interview with a researcher, Shirley Grainger, who has been investigating the working situation of actresses. For questions 22–34 answer the questions or complete the statements using one to three words. You will hear the piece twice.

INTERVIEWER: The results of a comprehensive statistical survey simply confirm what actresses have known for a long time – that there are fewer roles for women and that when actresses do work, they're less well paid than men and play younger roles. I spoke to Shirley Grainger who was asked by the Actors' Union to investigate the situation. What did her survey reveal?

SHIRLEY GRAINGER: The union was very concerned about all the anecdotal evidence they were getting when women were complaining that they were getting a raw deal and were not getting a proper chance to practise their art. But without hard evidence, which comes from a scientific investigation of the problem, it's very difficult to persuade the producers that there is a problem that they ought to be addressing. So, I had the task of getting the data together. To do this, I interviewed people from different branches of the profession, and was able to gather 35,000 pieces of information which I could then analyse.

INTERVIEWER: So what kind of information was this?

SHIRLEY GRAINGER: I got information about gender, age, types of role played and earnings, and I looked at people in the theatre, on TV and radio over a three year period. And the figures were really striking – I found differences between actors and actresses in all the fields surveyed, and these differences were significant statistically at a very high level. In TV for instance, men were twice as likely to be employed as women, but in radio that ratio went down even further, with women having only a one in three chance of getting an acting part when compared with men.

INTERVIEWER: Wow ...

SHIRLEY GRAINGER: Yes ... the other key finding was that women in the acting profession have their busiest working life in their twenties and thirties, whereas for men, the busiest time is when they're in their forties. And in fact, by the time they are forty, women drop out of radio and TV altogether.

INTERVIEWER: Well, these are really startling findings, aren't they? I mean, they do confirm what lots of people have been saying, but it's quite something to get this information in black and white.

SHIRLEY GRAINGER: Yes, and of course, that was precisely the role of the survey to provide firm evidence. Another important thing is pay. The rates of pay in radio, for example, are based on experience, so as long as there are fewer parts for women, this creates a vicious circle. There are far fewer parts for women, so they have less chance to gain experience. Then, when a woman does manage to get a part, she's paid less to do it.

INTERVIEWER: So what do producers feel about this situation?

SHIRLEY GRAINGER: They have tended to argue that in terms of pay, once women get the work, there is equality of treatment and they get paid the same, but our findings prove that this is not the case. In 95 per cent of the cases, women came off worse than men. This new information means that the union will now be able to argue a much stronger case.

INTERVIEWER: But women can only work if the parts are written for them...

SHIRLEY GRAINGER: Of course, and here there's a bit of passing the buck. The producers say they are just choosing material that reflects the world and the way it is. They make the point, and I don't know how valid this is, that dramatic situations are more likely to be found in the world of work, particularly in dangerous professions, where they argue men are still in the majority. Then they blame the writers, who they say don't write enough parts for women, especially plum parts. The poor writers say they don't have any power anyway, and so they can't be expected to initiate change. On radio, the audience figures show there's a 55 to 45 per cent ratio of women to men listening in the afternoon when a lot of drama goes out, so there's a pretty clear case for providing drama that caters to this particular group. But it doesn't mean that these dramas necessarily need to have a domestic context.

INTERVIEWER: So in practical terms how do you hope the union is going to use your findings?

SHIRLEY GRAINGER: Well, it seems that one simple thing that producers can be encouraged to do is to monitor the use of actors and actresses, and then look at these figures in comparison with the sort of figures they would like to be seeing. A more equitable profession is something many actresses would welcome. Also in new plays, where the cast list indicates a profession – be it a nurse, detective, judge and so on, producers could consider what gender this role should be. There's no reason for rigid stereotyping these days. Without this sort of monitoring it's difficult to see how any change is likely to come about. The union will have to be consistent in its pressure for there to be an effect.

SECTION D

You will hear five short extracts in which different people talk about losing jobs. You will hear the series twice.

In **Task one** *Letters A–H list the professions of the different people. As you listen, indicate who is speaking by completing the boxes numbered 35–39 with the appropriate letter.*

In **Task two** *Letters I–P list different facts about the people speaking in the five extracts. As you listen, put them in order by completing the boxes numbered 40–44 with the appropriate letter.*

1
I was called into the office of our new Managing Director and told that I was no longer required. I had no reason to suppose that my work had any cause for dissatisfaction – I mean my typing was always up to scratch and I knew from my friends that I was a popular person in the office. But the company had introduced lots of new equipment – word-processors, personal computers and so on so the executives didn't need so much back-up – they could prepare and print their own reports. I felt as if I'd completely lost control of my work situation. Like lots of people, I'm buying my house on a mortgage and I've had to reschedule repayments to the bank now that there's no money coming in. I'm just hoping I'll find something soon.

2
One of the things to recognise in this situation is that you are going to feel a bit up and down – and that's quite normal – but there's a lot you can do to minimise the transition from having a job to not having one. The first thing to do is to get yourself organised, you know, set up a room in your house as a sort of headquarters or office, make sure your filing system is right, all this will give you a boost. Make sure you structure your day, and start off by getting up

at the usual time and taking care with your appearance. That's one of the first things that people let go, and it's a big mistake.

3
Everyone in the agency was aware there'd been problems going on and over the months there'd been a reduction in the number of accounts I was responsible for. I mean, with the recession and everything, companies just didn't seem to want to spend so much on promoting their products. Anyway, the director called us in and said that the company was finished, it had gone bust, and we'd all have to go that very day. And we thought, well, this won't be too bad, we'll get some redundancy money, but he said, no, there wouldn't be any and we'd just have to try to get some money from government funds. It still hasn't sunk in yet. I don't know how I'm going to manage.

4
Of course like other firms, I find my company just doesn't have so many vacancies to fill in the present economic climate but yes, we do try to be fair when we've got jobs to offer, and we don't look unfavourably on applicants just because they've been out of work for more than a year. If they've got the qualifications we're looking for and can put together a persuasive curriculum vitae, we'll give them the benefit of the doubt and get them to come along for an interview. We're always on the lookout for people who've seen redundancy as a positive step, something that gives them a kick-start for new opportunities.

5
I landed this big part in a long-running serial which went out three times a week and I was in front of the cameras for nine consecutive months – pretty good experience for a novice like me – but the end came pretty swiftly. The show was going down in the ratings and the powers that be decided we were for the chop and the show came off within a month. After that I spent six months "resting" before anything at all came up. Quite a change of lifestyle I can tell you, with no money at all coming in.

PAPER 5 SPEAKING (15 minutes)

PHASE A (approximately 3 minutes)

The two examiners and two candidates introduce themselves to each other and exchange basic information about each other.

If the candidates do not already know each other, they may be asked to talk to each other to find out about the other person's life.

If the candidates do know each other, then each candidate may be asked to tell the examiners about the other person.

TEST 1

Areas covered are based on usual general topics when people first meet, such as where people come from, what they are currently doing (e.g. jobs and studying), where they are now living, what their likes and dislikes are.

PHASE B1 (approximately 2 minutes)

CHILDREN AND CARS (describe and relate)

One of the examiners gives each candidate a photograph of children and cars (on p.118 and p.125), telling them that the photographs are similar but not the same. Candidate A has one minute in which to describe the photograph to Candidate B as fully as possible, describing what the photograph shows and indicating how suitable the car is for use with the children.

Candidate B listens to Candidate A, and then says how their picture relates to Candidate A's picture, and says briefly what the idea is behind the two pictures (approximately twenty seconds).

The candidates then look together at both pictures and compare them.

PHASE B2 (approximately 2 minutes)

COASTAL LANDSCAPES (describe and identify)

One examiner gives each candidate a set of eight numbered photographs (p.121) to look at, with instructions not to look at each other's photos.

Candidate B is asked to describe *one* photograph in as much detail as possible so that Candidate A can identify which photograph has been described.

Candidate A is asked to listen to Candidate B, and after approximately one minute is then asked to identify the photograph.

Then both candidates compare the photographs.

PHASE C (3 or 4 minutes)

A WEEK'S DIET (evaluate and discuss)

Candidate A and candidate B together look at p.119 showing a week's menu.

They should give their opinion about the food in the pictures, and comment on how appropriate they think this type of food would be for a man doing a hard physical job, a woman who has a busy job outside the home and a child aged 10. They should also suggest any changes they think should be made to this diet.

PHASE D (3 or 4 minutes)

The examiners will now participate in the discussion and ask both candidates to comment further on the material from Phase C and then bring the interview to a close.

Test 2

ANSWER KEY

PAPER 1 READING

FIRST TEXT

1 F **2** C or E **3** E or C **4** B **5** A **6** D **7** E or F **8** F or E **9** E **10** D
11 D or E **12** E or D **13** A **14** E **15** B or F **16** F or B **17** C **18** A
19 B or C **20** C or B

SECOND TEXT

21 A **22** D **23** C **24** B **25** D **26** D **27** D **28** B **29** A **30** C

THIRD TEXT

31 C **32** F **33** A **34** D **35** B

FOURTH TEXT

36 C **37** A **38** B **39** D **40** C **41** A **42** D **43** A or B **44** B or A **45** C **46** B
47 C

PAPER 2 WRITING

Notes for guidance

SECTION A

1a This letter will have to be very tactful and you may not want to make your suspicions absolutely clear. You will, however, have to convey to Fiona that the situation is going to get worse not better. Note that 'Mick' is a diminutive form of 'Michael' and that the phone number in the advertisement is the same as the one that Fiona gives.

b Your note to Michael must ensure that he meets you, so you should write in general terms and not arouse his suspicions.

SECTION B

2 This is an informal letter. Start 'Dear (name of friend – choose one). You can end with 'Best Wishes' then sign your first name. Mention one pet only and describe how to look after it in some detail. Refer to your own experience. Make sure that you cover every point in the question – care, food, advantages and disadvantages.

3 This is a formal letter (Dear Sir or Madam + Yours faithfully). Mention the activities that you believe would be most popular and say why. Be realistic and base your answer on your own experience of such centres. You can mention such facilities as a café, shop, etc.

4 This is a report and should start like this:
TO:
FROM:
SUBJECT:
DATE:

You should divide the report into sections, each with its own heading, e.g. Recent Problems, The Meeting, Recommendations. You should report what was said at the meeting and make recommendations about preventing theft and vandalism. The recommendations could be summarised in a list at the end of the report.

5 Book reviews normally have the title of the book and the name of the author (and sometimes the publisher and price) at the top of the review. They should provide readers with a clear idea of the content, and your reactions to it. Remember to include the name of the book and its author.

PAPER 3 ENGLISH IN USE

SECTION A

1   1 A   2 D   3 B   4 A   5 C   6 C   7 B   8 D   9 A   10 B   11 C   12 D   13 C
        14 A   15 B

2   16 do   17 such/these   18 no/little   19 which   20 less/smaller   21 is   22 of
        23 although/though   24 back   25 by/through   26 just   27 is   28 makes
        29 among   30 which/that

SECTION B

3   31 kind   32 ✔   33 than   34 they   35 to   36 its   37 do   38 ✔   39 ✔
        40 then   41 them   42 being   43 have   44 are   45 should

TEST 2

4 **46** in advance/beforehand **47** pounds/money/currency **48** refund/pay back **49** at least/more than **50** impassable/blocked **51** wise/sensible/advisable **52** arrive **53** leave/depart **54** come next **55** all right/OK **56** jump/sit **57** only **58** (very) seriously **59** drive **60** your own/some/enough

SECTION C

5 **61** B **62** H **63** I **64** F **65** C

6 (Model answers)

66 After graduating from Sydney University in 1905 he became a lecturer in mineralogy and geology at Adelaide University, where he worked for the rest of his life but he did not spend all his time in the academic atmosphere of a university.

67 He went on his first Antarctic expedition in 1905–7 and returned in 1911 as the leader of the Australian Antarctic Expedition.

68 In 1912, when he was 315 miles from base camp, one of his two companions died when he drove the sledge containing most of the food into a deep crevasse.

69 Mawson and his remaining companion, Xavier Mertz, had to kill and eat their huskie dogs in order to survive.

70 Both began to suffer from a mysterious illness, from which Mertz died, leaving Mawson to travel alone for 28 days, desperately ill and starving before he eventually reached base camp.

71 Doctors could not explain Mawson's illness, from which he made a rapid recovery, but many years later scientists realised that both explorers had suffered from vitamin A poisoning caused by eating the liver of the huskie dogs.

72 Despite the physical hardships he endured, Mawson led another major expedition to Antarctica from 1929–31 and lived until 1958.

PAPER 4 LISTENING

SECTION A

1 £45 **2** a year's wages **3** in country houses
4 manual exchanges
5 reduction in cost   } (in any order)
6 increase in numbers
7 through the operator **8** 1970's/1975 **9** slow/unreliable
10 unreliable/slow

TEST 2

SECTION B

11 engine sheds **12** telegraph office **13** post office **14** Fairbourne (born/e) **15** ferry
16 Italy **17** 10.45 **18** horse-drawn/electric **19** electric/horse-drawn
20 teddy (bear)

SECTION C

21 C **22** B **23** A **24** C **25** C **26** B **27** C **28** C

SECTION D

Task one
29 H **30** B **31** C **32** G **33** F

Task two
34 N **35** L **36** M **37** I **38** J

TAPESCRIPT

SECTION A

You will hear someone talking to a group of people about the development of the telephone. Listen to the recording and fill in the information for questions 1–10 with an appropriate word or short phrase. You do not need to write full sentences. You will hear the recording twice.

PRESENTER: Welcome everyone to our monthly meeting. I know you've all been looking forward to the chance to hear tonight's guest speaker, Tom Wilkinson, who's going to talk to us about the history of telephones. So without more ado, Tom Wilkinson.

TOM WILKINSON: Good evening, ladies and gentlemen. It gives me great pleasure to be here tonight to talk about a subject that has fascinated me for many years, the telephone and how it works.

These days, when you dial a friend in Australia, it's easy to take the whole thing for granted. After a few clicks and whirrs, you're through. Thousands of miles vanish in an instant. It's so easy. But anyone over fifty will remember a time when it could take hours to phone a friend just a few hundred miles away. In fact, if we take a brief look at the development of the phone system, we'll find that not much changed at all between 1880 and 1950.

TEST 2

In 1880, when the first brass and mahogany phone arrived, it cost £45, the equivalent of a year's wages for the average working man. In those far off days, the airwaves were virtually silent. There were no exchanges in Britain and most of the telephones in use were installed in large country houses so the wealthy could talk to their servants and each other.

By the 1920's, there were manual exchanges in towns and cities up and down the country, the cost of telephones had come down considerably and far more of us were installing the new wonder instrument. But by 1930, there were still only a few experimental automatic exchanges. This meant that all calls had to go through an operator. When you picked up the receiver the operator was automatically alerted at the exchange: basically a little flap dropped on her switchboard or a light came on and she knew you wanted to use the phone. With the Magneto telephone, the only alternative to the standard model, you cranked a handle on the side of the phone to alert the operator who then rang you to ask what number you wanted.

The system then, and it lasted into the 1970s in some areas, was that the operator would decide how to route your call. She would contact the next exchange on your route and the operator at that exchange would either connect you or hand you on to what could turn out to be the first in a whole series of operators, depending on how far your call had to go. And if one of the exchanges on the way happened to be engaged, you simply had to wait until it cleared. Incredibly, the last manual exchange was still operating in Abingdon, Oxfordshire, as late as 1975. People in the area still had phones without dials and all their calls had to be put through, manually, by the operator.

How things have changed! Today a lightning-fast, digital system works out how to route your call in a split second and a call from London to Oxford may go via Edinburgh if all the more direct routes are engaged. Such is the speed of modern technology that we notice no delay.

In an emergency, the old system was horribly slow and not always reliable. But there was something rather grand about the stately progress of a call that could only be achieved through the skills of a series of individual operators devoting their energies to keeping you in touch.

SECTION B

You will hear an ansaphone recording announcing details of rail and steam attractions at the weekend. For questions 11–20, make notes to complete the information. Note that some details have been completed for you. Listen very carefully because you will hear this piece only once.

Thank you for calling the special info line with details of special Rail and Steam attractions this August weekend. We've got three attractions to tell you about, at Swanley, Fairbourne and Matlock.

Attraction number one is the Central Railway at Swanley. Step back in time on this steam railway that will take you on an hour's trip through unspoilt countryside. Especially recommended for children over five who will enjoy the chance after the train ride, to visit the engine sheds and see the old steam trains collected here from different parts of the country. How did telegraph systems work? Here's your opportunity to find out in the working re-creation of a telegraph office where visitors can operate the equipment, and there's a post office where the kids can help sort the parcels as they come off the train in the delivery area. Sundays only, ten to six, adults £5, children £2.50.

The second attraction is the Fairbourne Connection, a narrow-gauge railway that runs for ten miles along the seashore, passing through stations over a hundred years old, two of which have recently been restored to their former glory. Many visitors are tempted to take the short ferry connection across the bay to Henderson Island where they can visit a village built in Italian style. There's an open-air restaurant and gardens to enjoy. One train only per day at 10.45 from Fairbourne station. Adults £7.50, children free.

What do you know about trams? Our third suggestion for steam enthusiasts is a trip to a Tramway Museum at Matlock where there's a collection of restored horse-drawn, steam and electric trams. All rides are free once you've paid the entrance fee, and you can have as many rides as you like. This weekend is a special teddy bear weekend and any child bringing an adult and a teddy will be allowed in free. The route covers a one-mile scenic track, and if the weather's not up to much, there are models to play with and a video to watch on the history of the tram.

Entrance fee £6.50 per adult, £2 for accompanying children.

SECTION C

You will hear a radio interview with a person who is blind. For questions 21–28 choose the most suitable answer, A, B, C or D. You will hear the piece twice.

JENNY WHITE: In the third of my occasional series, 'How do they do it?', I talked to James Hanbury, who's been blind since the age of three, about how he views the world. I asked him first about how his blindness came about.

JAMES: I suffered from a rare condition, but at least it's a well-understood phenomenon. It's a tumour which attacks the retina. Even when the tumour is removed, it quite often leads to further complications, but if you survive into your teens, you're more or less safe.

JENNY WHITE: So do you have any vision at all?

JAMES: No, I don't see at all. Some people, even people who are totally blind, retain some kind of visual concept, but I really have none. So I have only the understanding of the visual world which I have been able to acquire by listening and learning how other people live. I am in a world where there is no light, no colour and no shape.

JENNY WHITE: So how does this affect you?

JAMES: One of the problems about being blind is getting out of yourself and getting across to other people. And even if you are a person with lots of ideas and you know how to conduct a conversation and so on, you can miss the fact that the person you're talking to looks awful because they've got flu, or has a wonderful suntan and have obviously been somewhere terrific – so you don't think of saying : 'Gosh, where have you been?'

That's the difficulty about being blind. However intelligent and creative you are, you are working with a very limited palette. People imagine that if you can't see, you also can't hear and can't think. There is some truth in this, because so much of hearing actually depends on the organisation of sight. It isn't true that blind people have got very sharp ears and always know what's going on; in fact, sight is the central organising sense, and so not being able to see makes it difficult to use your ears as intelligently as you would like. Consequently, blind people often find it difficult to tell what is going on when there are a large number of people in a place. It's difficult to keep your end up.

JENNY WHITE: Yes, I can appreciate that.

JAMES: And, you know, if you're the sort of person who as a matter of course knocks over tables laden with china or causes similar physical calamities, you must learn to take it without letting it knock you off balance. I think that if I can learn how to keep calm, other people will take their lead from me: an indiscreet show of anxiety or panic doesn't help people to conquer their fear of blind people.

JENNY WHITE: So you really learn to pick up on how others are feeling ...

JAMES: Well, yes. Of course it makes quite a difference not seeing someone, but one does become skilled in body language: it's extra-sensory. One grows skilled in listening to develop a high level of perception. That's not to say one isn't influenced by what a third party may say. I may be getting to know someone and then my wife or a colleague will say: 'Oh, I can't stand that person, he never looks at you,' or: 'He never smiles.' I've often been caught out with that one about smiling. I'm always interested to hear whether someone is attractive.

JENNY WHITE: Tell me about your schooldays. How did you relate to people then?

JAMES: I was totally segregated when I was at school, which was something I find very hard to forgive. It was extremely damaging. One of the arguments for it is you concentrate resources by segregating handicapped children, but I don't think anything can outweigh the social disadvantages and the intellectual isolation which come about as a result of segregation. I found it really difficult to adjust to living in the real world and mixing with ordinary people.

JENNY WHITE: Do you think things have improved now for people in a similar condition to yours?

JAMES: I'd like to say I believe things are changing for the better – all around me I see blind people who are working very hard at finding a better life for themselves. The most important change since I was at school is that there is now a strong move towards integration of blind children in mainstream education. As social integration grows, sighted people are exposed much more to blind people, and I think that's breaking down prejudice.

JENNY WHITE: You've got a responsible job. Is that a source of pride?

JAMES: I would really rather be doing something else – I'm not really happy teaching. I'm not at all interested in computers, I just happen to know about them because I was a computer programmer for a long time, and also, having been a teacher, I've got the pedagogic tradition, so I know how to put the course together. I'm also not at all happy about teaching blind people. I think I'm pretty well settled to the fact that my mark in life is not going to be in my career. That's a pity, but I'm reconciled to that now.

I'm trying to put together a book at the moment. In a sense, the last thing I want to do is write about being blind, because that would be the least integrative thing I could do. I do think about other things as well, but I find increasingly as I get older that I can't really turn my mind to the other things until I find some way of answering the basic questions about blindness, and there are an awful lot of them. It may well be that writing a book, as for so many people, is a therapeutic experience – I don't know. I'm a bit of a pessimist, you see, and as I get older I actually think blindness is more difficult to cope with. You become technically more capable as a middle-aged person, but I think actually the tragedy of it becomes more difficult to bear.

SECTION D

You will hear five short extracts in which different people talk about performing in public.

*In **Task one** letters A–H list the professions of the different people. As you listen, indicate who is speaking by completing the boxes numbered 29–33 with the appropriate letter.*

TEST 2

*In **Task two** letters I–P list things the people speaking in the five extracts did. Write the appropriate letter in the boxes beside the speakers, numbered 34–38.*

1

The physical effect of nerves on the body can be absolutely shattering for those who perform in public. Why should this be so? Well, if you have always been under pressure, and you've never admitted it, you've just gone on looking and sounding good, then one day the nervous system can just collapse. It just says I can't take it any more. The fear of letting people down becomes too much.

2

I had actually played this particular concerto many, many times before, but on this particular occasion, I really don't know why, it was such a nerve-racking experience. We'd had the usual rehearsals with the orchestra and they'd gone really well. So, on the night, I arrived, bowed, sat down, it came to my turn to perform, I looked at the keyboard. And I was just gripped by terror. I found that my knees were knocking, my neck ached, I couldn't see properly, it was as if I wasn't there. I just didn't know what I was supposed to be doing.

3

I think it's a bit different for me and for some other people. I mean, if you're a trumpet player, or a singer or an actor, then you have to do it to script. When you're speaking, as I have to do when I'm defending someone in court, or if I've been asked to speak at a conference, you know all the points you want to put forward but you can do them in any order you like. However with playing you've actually got to do it when it says you've got to do it and that's what causes the nerves, you see your bit coming up, and you think, oh no, I can never do this.

4

My cue is getting nearer, I'm not going to be able to go on, I know I'm not going to be able to go on. I'm stuck here. My shoes have been stuck to the floor. Doesn't anybody understand this? I'm all alone. No one can help me. I'm going to walk out into that spotlight and everyone is going to know. How can this happen to me, after all these years. And the others, my fellow players. They must keep their side of the bargain. They mustn't look at me, they mustn't look me in the eyes or I'm done for.

5

I wasn't playing the trumpet at the time, I think I was filling in on side drums and I took these tranquillisers, not many, and I found myself very relaxed, very relaxed indeed, in fact too relaxed, and I remember well when we were playing in the concert. I should have been playing the side-drum going *bom bu bu bom*, something like that and instead of that I was going *bu bu bu bom* and I was happily banging away doing this and the conductor looked across at me and he was looking at me very strangely emphasising his beat, looking very hard at me and I thought, 'He wants me to play louder', and being very relaxed about it on these tranquillisers I started to play louder and louder and of course it was all wrong, he was trying to tell me, you know, get it right.

PAPER 5 SPEAKING (15 minutes)

PHASE A

(See p.25–26)

PHASE B1 (approximately 2 minutes)

PEOPLE AND ROOMS (describe and contrast)

One of the examiners gives each candidate a photograph of a person in a room (p.118 and p.125), telling them that the photographs are similar but not the same.

Candidate A has one minute to describe their photograph to Candidate B as fully as possible, describing what the photograph shows and what he/she thinks the room shows about the character of the person whose room it is.

Candidate B listens to Candidate A, and then says how their picture is different from Candidate A's (approximately twenty seconds).

The candidates then look together at both pictures and compare them.

PHASE B2 (approximately 2 minutes)

CLOCKS (describe and draw)

Candidate B is given a set of eight drawings of different types of clock (p.117) and is asked to choose *one* for candidate A to draw. About one minute is allowed for this description.

At the end of one minute, the candidates compare the photographs and the drawing.

PHASE C (3 or 4 minutes)

MOBILE PHONES (evaluate and rank order)

Candidate A and B together will be shown p.128 containing a number of photographs of people using mobile phones. They should discuss how useful they think such a phone is to each of the people depicted in the photographs, and put the people in

TEST 2

order, with the person to whom it is most useful occurring first, and the person to whom it is least useful last.

PHASE D (3 or 4 minutes)

The examiners will now participate in the discussion and ask both candidates to comment further on the material from phase C and then bring the interview to a close.

Test 3

ANSWER KEY

PAPER 1 READING

FIRST TEXT

1 D 2 A 3 B 4 A 5 B 6 D 7 C 8 A 9 B 10 D 11 C 12 A
13 C 14 D 15 A 16 D

SECOND TEXT

17 C 18 B 19 C 20 C 21 C 22 D

THIRD TEXT

23 G 24 E 25 B 26 F 27 A 28 D

FOURTH TEXT

29 B 30 C 31 A 32 C 33 D 34 C or D 35 D or C 36 B 37 D 38 C 39 B
40 C

PAPER 2 WRITING

Notes for guidance

SECTION A

1a Remember how to set out a report (see p.29). Use the numbers in the questionnaire to make general points, e.g. 'Most students thought ... Nearly everybody thinks ...'

b Since this is intended for a notice-board, it must have a heading that attracts people's attention. Write short sentences and paragraphs.

SECTION B

2 A leaflet, like a notice, must have a heading that catches the reader's attention. You must write persuasively, since you want people to give you things. Make sure

TEST 3

that you cover every point in the question. You should put your name and position at the end of the leaflet.

3 This is an informal letter to a friend and should be reassuring in tone. Make practical and sensible suggestions.

4 This is an informal letter. Make sure that you cover every aspect mentioned in the question. Your letter must make recommendations about protecting the house and personal safety.

5 Think of a headline for your article. You could have a series of sub-headings or questions, e.g. *What was the happiest moment in your life?/The happiest moment in my life,* followed by short answers. You can write a serious or a humorous article.

PAPER 3 USE OF ENGLISH

SECTION A

1 1 A 2 C 3 B 4 A 5 B 6 C 7 B 8 A 9 D 10 C 11 A 12 D 13 B 14 A 15 D

2 16 from 17 such 18 deal/amount 19 able 20 some/certain 21 but 22 will/can 23 when/if 24 without 25 which 26 like 27 to 28 another 29 because/as/since 30 at/for

SECTION B

3 31 just 32 they 33 of 34 it 35 ✔ 36 how 37 organised 38 be 39 ✔ 40 the 41 regard 42 themselves 43 ✔ 44 so 45 the

4 46 fortnight 47 exciting/interesting/adventurous/different/outdoor
48 previous experience 49 you need/you require/required/needed/necessary
50 a few 51 the end 52 been before/been already/tried it/done it 53 last
54 go again/re-apply 55 enclosed 56 free 57 advantage 58 good enough
59 how well/about what 60 losing

SECTION C

5 61 E 62 H 63 F 64 C 65 A

6 (Model answers)

66 In 1783 Sebastian le Normand, who invented the word 'parachute', made a safe descent from the tower of Montpellier Observatory and four years later Jaques Garnerin jumped from a balloon 1,000 metres over Paris.

67 Garnerin later demonstrated his parachute, which unlike modern parachutes had a rigid canopy and a small basket to stand in, all over Europe and in 1836 his niece, Eliza, became the first woman parachutist.

68 Because these early parachutists descended from balloons it did not matter how big the parachute was but with the invention of aeroplanes it became important to design a parachute that was small enough to be worn by a pilot.

69 Various parachutes of that type were in use in the early twentieth century but the one that forms the basis for all modern designs was invented by Leslie Irvin and demonstrated by him in 1919.

70 It soon became normal practice for pilots to wear parachutes and so far more than 130,000 lives have been saved in both civil and military flying.

71 At first parachutes were thought of as a means of saving lives in an emergency but by the 1930s many countries had parachute regiments, usually regarded as an elite, as part of their armed forces.

72 Even in Garnerin's time parachuting was an exciting activity that attracted adventurous people and today it is a popular sport all over the world.

PAPER 4 LISTENING

SECTION A

1 LA 405 **2** Impulse **3** Never Satisfied **4** Impulse **5** LA 405
6 Impulse **7** LA 405 **8** Never Satisfied **9** LA 405 **10** Never Satisfied

SECTION B

11 Dr John Smith **12** 37 King Street **13** 0454-46-29-93
14 13th January **15** 1SMI 14 **16** order incomplete **17** DC10-5V adaptor

SECTION C

18 'You and Your Handwriting' **19** selection procedures
20 ambition
21 sensitivity to others } (in any order)
22 broad-mindedness
23 the expense **24** executive posts **25** slope(or slant)/it's erratic
26 it's erratic/slope(or slant) **27** the job interview

TEST 3

28 she doesn't accept the research evidence

29 they are afraid of losing their jobs

SECTION D

Task one

30 C   **31** F   **32** E   **33** H   **34** A

Task two

35 J   **36** L   **37** K   **38** M   **39** N

TAPESCRIPT

SECTION A

You will hear someone talking about electric cars, past and present. Listen to the recording and for questions 1–10, put a tick in the appropriate column to indicate which car each statement refers to. You will hear the recording twice.

What will motoring be like in the twenty-first century? Well, as far as a number of manufacturers are concerned, it may well lie with the electric car, powered by a battery. This may sound innovative, or even futuristic, but in actual fact the electric car had its moment of glory as long ago as 1899. That was the year in which a Belgian driver, Camille Jenatzy, achieved the land speed record of over a hundred kilometres an hour while driving his battery-powered racing car in France. This really was a sensation because at the time there was no petrol-driven car that could manage anything like that speed. In order to achieve his feat, Jenatzy, whose car was named 'Never Satisfied' if you translate its name into English, made use of the key feature of battery-powered cars that exists to this day – the fact that you can either travel a relatively long distance at a very modest speed or a very short distance at high speed. The latter was what Jenatzy went for.

So electric cars have been around for a long time, even if they haven't made much impact on the market. But today they are gaining prominence as a result of recent legislation in Los Angeles. In polluted California, legislators have decided that two per cent of cars must be 'zero emission' vehicles. To you, me and the manufacturers, that means cutting down on exhaust fumes and there's something of a rush to produce suitable vehicles. I'm going to tell you about two of them.

The first isn't a pure electric car, it's a hybrid. The LA 405, development of which is partly funded by a £4m grant from Los Angeles City Authority, has two motors, a 45 kilowatt electric unit and a tiny petrol engine. It has a maximum speed of 120 kilometres per hour and can accelerate to 80 kilometres per hour in about 17 seconds. The battery range allows you to travel for around 90 kilometres before recharging, and the petrol engine increases that range by another 140 kilometres. This car even has air-conditioning, run through solar panels on the roof. This neat solution avoids the problem of draining the battery by making too heavy a demand on it. Recharging is easy: You either plug into the mains at night, or during the day while the car is parked – Los Angeles is installing recharge points in Los Angeles's car parks and shopping malls.

The General Car Company is developing its electric car, called Impulse. The Impulse has a power pack composed of 32 lead-acid batteries, which drive two electric motors, one for each front wheel. Its top speed is 160 kilometres per hour and it is capable of 0 to 95 kilometres in eight seconds, a respectable pace for a petrol-driven car. The breakthrough with this car is in the electronic unit, which converts DC current to AC current, allowing more efficient use of power.

At the moment, electric cars continue to proliferate, and a number of European producers have got in on the act, but mostly they are exploratory prototypes; very few actually reach the market. Who knows what our roads will look like when they do?

SECTION B

You will hear an ansaphone message left by a customer at Purvis and Company. Look at the form below and fill in the information for questions 11–17. Some of the information has been provided for you. Listen very carefully as you will hear this piece only once.

Hello. Thank you for calling Purvis and Company, the firm that deals with everything you need for state of the art computer software. I am afraid there is no one in the office at the moment who can take your call but if you leave a message with details of your name, contact number and the nature of your enquiry, we will get back to you as soon as possible. Please speak immediately after you hear the tone.

My name is Dr John Smith and I live at 37 King Street, Marsham, Gloucestershire, telephone 0454-46-29-93. I rang two weeks ago about your Stand Alone Modem FM 2500. I ordered this model by telephone on the 13th January and paid by credit card (customer order number 16439; date of invoicing 14th January; invoice number 19292; sales person ML; customer code 1SM I 14. You sent me the modem by Express Courier and I received it the next day. So far, so good. But when I opened the parcel, the adaptor was missing. It's a DC10-5V adaptor and I can't use the modem without it – I can't even plug it in. I rang about this last week, and one of your staff – I don't remember his name – said he would send the adaptor by first class post the same day. I still have not received it and I need it urgently because I am setting up an electronic mail network with British and European universities. Will you please send this to me immediately? I've been in touch with the manufacturers, but they say I have to get this adaptor through you, as you are the dealers where the modem was purchased and you hold the guarantee for all relevant parts of the apparatus. I repeat, it's the DC10-5V adaptor that's missing. If you don't either return my call or despatch the equipment within forty-eight hours, I'll be taking this matter up with my solicitors.

SECTION C

You will hear a radio programme in which three people discuss the uses of graphology. For questions 18–29, complete the information using an appropriate word or short phrase. You will hear the piece twice.

BRIAN WESTON: When you apply for a job, how do you expect people to judge your suitability? Will they be looking at your qualifications? Or your previous experience in similar types of jobs? Well, the evidence is that more and more companies, in this country and abroad, are employing graphologists to study people's handwriting. And it's on the basis of their analysis that your psychological suitability for this post will be decided. How fair is this? I talked to two people, Tom Phelps, a practising graphologist and author of 'You and Your Handwriting', and Margot Sawyer, a psychologist at Brimscombe College, who has made a particular study of selection procedures and their effectiveness. So, Tom, what can you tell from looking at someone's handwriting?

TOM PHELPS: Well Brian, of course, handwriting reveals deep psychological traits – ambition, sensitivity to other people, how broad-minded you are, all sorts of things like that, but if we're going to talk today mainly about its role in job selection, then I'd also be looking for things that tell me about the applicant's current situation.

BRIAN WESTON: Such as what, exactly?

TOM PHELPS: Well, for executive jobs – and this is where graphology is mostly used, in this country anyway – a consultation is quite expensive so you only want to pay that sort of money for these high level appointments – handwriting can show quite clearly whether or not an applicant is under stress.

BRIAN WESTON: How does it do this?

TOM PHELPS: Well, basically, there's going to be quite a lot of variation in the slope, the slant of the writing. The handwriting will be quite erratic. You can also tell if someone is drinking too much, and how they relate to other people and their environment.

BRIAN WESTON: So it's a sort of …

TOM PHELPS: It's a pretty effective diagnostic tool, yes, certainly if you judge by the number of companies who are using graphologists in their selection procedures now.

BRIAN WESTON: Right, well all that sounds pretty conclusive to me. But what do you think, Margot?

MARGOT SAWYER: Yes, that's right, a number of companies are using this technique, but you know, the history of selection is peppered with techniques that don't work very well. I mean, the commonest form of selection is the interview, a one to one situation between employer and applicant, and over and over again this has been shown to be a very bad way of selecting people. Virtually all organisations use it, over 90 per cent in fact. So the argument that because firms do something it must be good just doesn't stand up really.

BRIAN WESTON: What are your objections to graphology as such then?

MARGOT SAWYER: Well, it's the job of psychologists to stand back and to look at techniques objectively, to see if they work empirically. And the research evidence shows overwhelmingly that this technique doesn't come up with what it's meant to. As an example of this, I could point to a typical study. Two graphologists were given samples of handwriting. These were taken from fifty employees in a telecommunications firm who were being assessed for promotion to managerial level within the company. Firstly, the graphologists didn't agree on their results, and secondly, both failed to predict the outcome of the selection procedure.

BRIAN WESTON: So there's no scientific evidence that it actually works?

TOM PHELPS: Well, as a graphologist, I could point to at least two studies that show that it does, one conducted in South Africa and another conducted in Israel. And you wouldn't have companies employing the costly services of graphologists year after year if they found what they did to be particularly useless.

MARGOT SAWYER: Yes, but if you look at the research evidence as a whole, you're obviously going to find one or two studies which actually point favourably to it. I'd have to say that any selection procedure is a bit like looking into a crystal ball. The proof of the success of a technique would be that you had actually identified those people really capable of doing the job. This would constitute the empirical proof, and there'd be a very strong case in favour of it.

TOM PHELPS: Look, in the US it's been proved that psychologists are strongly opposed to graphologists, for the simple reason that they're afraid they'll take over their jobs. And graphology is being used in therapy too now.

BRIAN WESTON: So are you afraid of being pushed out of a job, Margot?

TEST 3

MARGOT SAWYER: No, I'm not actually. Psychologists are less interested in graphology than in processes of selection. Firms ask us to come along and look at whether this is working in a particular organisation, and we evaluate the research and come up with a scientifically respectable conclusion.

BRIAN WESTON: And so the debate goes on …

SECTION D

You will hear five short extracts in which different people comment on their experiences of being prize winners. You will hear the series twice.

In **Task one** *Letters A–H list the different people. As you listen, indicate who is speaking by completing the boxes numbered 30–34 with the appropriate letter.*

In **Task two** *Letters I–P list different facts about the people speaking in the five extracts. As you listen, put them in order by completing the boxes numbered 35–39 with the appropriate letter.*

1

I went along to the Phoenix Theatre and stood on a vast stage and performed for about ten minutes in front of a panel of producers and directors. I'd chosen a speech from 'Romeo and Juliet' … anyway the next day the principal of the stage school called me in and told me I'd won the prize for the Best Drama Student and I thought, 'This is it' and so far it has been. The job offers have just kept pouring in.

2

For me the financial side wasn't what I entered for, although the winner of the Portrait Award does get £5000 in cash. I really just wanted to get some pictures into the exhibition, and the real carrot was the chance of a portrait commission that would go on permanent display in a prestigious art gallery. Winning the award was really just a start for me, and it's only now really that I'm beginning to do what I really want, large scale works in the figurative tradition. I'm simply fascinated by faces.

3

When I entered the competition, I was just seventeen and my horizons were focused on boyfriends and homework. But when I got through the preliminary heats and into the concerto final I felt really happy and relaxed. I just wanted to go out and communicate with the audience. My flute playing really seemed to appeal to them – and to the judges. Even so, I kept to my original plan and went to university to do a degree in English, and I'm glad of those years. I've got an international career as a soloist now but my academic training puts the jetsetting into perspective. You could say I've still got my feet very much on the ground.

4
The competition was held in Switzerland and was open to both boys and girls. For someone from my country where there isn't a strong ballet tradition and there's no national company, it was a chance to assess my talents against the young blood from other countries. I was impressed by the way some people moved, their technique was superb. I made a lot of contacts which were crucial and then as part of the prize I had the chance to give two performances in New York, which got me noticed. It led to the chance for further study and a contract with a leading classical company. Winning the competition was my passport. Without it I'd have gone straight into teaching and there would have been no prospect of a performing career.

5
When I was twelve, I won the under-fourteen cross-country championship and it all came so easily to me, I mean I just put on my trainers and shorts and you couldn't stop me wanting to go faster than anyone else. And I loved circuit training on the track. After the win there was a bit of a reaction and I found it difficult to settle down to school life. People had been telling me I was wonderful and real life seemed a bit of a comedown. I plodded on and eventually got an athletic scholarship to a college on the west coast in the States, and then I realised I was actually good at academic subjects and I went on to study law. I was too successful too young. Life's better now, there's a clearer sense of priorities.

PAPER 5 SPEAKING (15 minutes)

PHASE A

(See p.25–26)

PHASE B1 (approximately 2 minutes)

MOTHERS AND SONS (describe, relate and hypothesise)

One of the examiners gives each candidate a photograph of a mother and son (p.120 and p.126), telling them that the photographs are similar but not the same, and instructing them not to look at each other's photograph.

Candidate A has one minute in which to describe the photograph of the mother and schoolboy as fully as possible to Candidate B, describing what the photograph shows and indicating what he/she thinks is the relationship between the mother and son.

Candidate B listens to Candidate A, and then says how their photograph relates to Candidate A's photograph and how the relationship between the mother and son in their photograph might be different (approximately twenty seconds).

The candidates together look at both photographs and hypothesise about them.

TEST 3

PHASE B2 (approximately 2 minutes)

CAKES (describe and eliminate)

Candidates A and B look at p.123 containing photographs of eight cakes. Candidate B has one minute in which to describe *five* of the cakes, so that Candidate A will be able to identify which *three* of the eight cakes have *not* been described.

After one minute, Candidate A is asked to identify the three photographs and then both candidates compare pictures.

PHASE C (3 or 4 minutes)

OIL SPILL (hypothesise and discuss)

Candidates A and B will each be given a photograph of an oil spill on a rocky coastline (p.122) and asked to discuss what they consider the consequences of the spill will be to the sea, to the wildlife and to the people in the area affected. They should also suggest what should be done to clean up the effects of the oil.

PHASE D (3 or 4 minutes)

The examiners will now participate in the discussion and ask both candidates to comment further on the material from Phase C and then bring the interview to a close.

Test 4

ANSWER KEY

PAPER 1 READING

FIRST TEXT

1 A 2 C 3 B 4 A 5 C 6 D 7 B 8 B 9 A 10 D or C 11 C or D 12 A
13 D 14 C 15 D 16 A or B 17 B or A 18 C 19 B 20 C

SECOND TEXT

21 D 22 B 23 B 24 D 25 B 26 D

THIRD TEXT

27 E 28 B 29 F 30 A 31 D

FOURTH TEXT

32 E 33 F 34 H 35 B 36 C
37 D 38 D 39 A 40 C

PAPER 2 WRITING

Notes for guidance

SECTION A

1a You may choose to write this as a formal or informal letter. The purpose of the letter is to rearrange the timetable in the light of the information in the telephone message, so your letter should include the new timetable. You may firmly but politely complain about the inconvenience of doing this. Alternatively, you may decide to cancel the entire tournament.

b This is a formal letter. Begin 'Dear Sir Philip' and end 'Yours sincerely'. Sir Philip may not be able to fit in with your new plans. You must offer him the chance to do so but also suggest an alternative – such as meeting the players at dinner but not awarding the prizes, or you may decide to have two prize-giving ceremonies at different times. What you say in **a** and **b** must be consistent.

TEST 4

SECTION B

2 Lay out your answer as a report (see p.29). Remember the things that business people appreciate in hotels, e.g. Fax, secretarial services, photocopying, meeting rooms, a well-stocked bar.

3 This is an informal letter. It should be reassuring in tone.

4 This is a formal letter (Dear Sir or Madam + Yours faithfully). You must make a clear choice and give reasons. If you choose the one-year stay, you should mention a specific country and language.

5 An advertisement needs an eye-catching heading. You must list exactly ten items with short, attractive descriptions and include all the information mentioned in the question. Be precise and include plenty of detail, e.g. 'Sonic the Hedgehog II for Sega Gamegear' rather than 'a computer game'.

PAPER 3 ENGLISH IN USE

SECTION A

1 1 A 2 B 3 C 4 D 5 B 6 C 7 A 8 D 9 A 10 A 11 D 12 A 13 A 14 B 15 D

2 16 had/reached/achieved 17 for 18 of 19 a 20 It 21 enough 22 may/might 23 this/the 24 it 25 much 26 could 27 This 28 its/the/his 29 their 30 them

SECTION B

3 31 lose 31 ✓ 33 choose 34 receive 35 travel 36 frightening 37 ✓ 38 advice 39 ✓ 40 loan 41 success 42 case 43 ✓ 44 . At 45 whether

4 46 wealthy/well-off/rich/affluent 47 manager 48 Each 49 waved 50 trembling/shaking 51 hand over/give them 52 floor 53 bit 54 close 55 teeth 56 confused 57 taking anything/any money/The money 58 drove off/drove away 59 immediately/quickly 60 will recover

SECTION C

5 61 F 62 G 63 A 64 C 65 B

6 (Model answers)

66 Gold does not easily react with other substances, is unaffected by temperature changes and resists acids.

67 Half of the world's gold is mined in South Africa and there are also large deposits in Russia but only tiny amounts in Britain.

68 Pure gold is said to have 24 carats but this is rather soft, so gold used for jewellery has 18 or 22 carats because it has been mixed with other metals, usually copper, to strengthen it.

69 Apart from jewellery, gold is used by dentists because it is safe to put it inside the human body and by scientists and engineers who value its special characteristics.

70 The desire for gold was an important stimulus to European exploration of America in the 16th and 17th centuries and in the 19th century there was a big gold rush in California in 1849 and in Australia in 1851, both of which led to rapid increases in population in those areas.

71 In Australia in 1872 a single gold nugget of 214 kilograms was found, the largest ever, which, after refining, gave 85 kilograms of pure gold.

72 Although governments no longer support their currencies with gold or have gold coins in circulation, central banks in all countries keep very large stocks of gold in well-protected vaults.

PAPER 4 LISTENING

SECTION A

1 A   **2** C   **3** D   **4** F   **5** H   **6** I

SECTION B

7 6,786   **8** 38   **9** 43   **10** 687   **11** 24 hours 37 mins   **12** 2   **13** 0.1   **14** 26,000

SECTION C

15 M   **16** MR   **17** R   **18** M   **19** RM   **20** R   **21** M   **22** M

SECTION D

Task one
23 D   **24** G   **25** C   **26** H   **27** B

Task two
28 P   **29** L   **30** J   **31** N   **32** K

TEST 4

TAPESCRIPT

SECTION A

You will hear a short description of a traffic accident. Some of the pictures below illustrate events in the accident, mentioned by the speaker and some do not. If a picture fits the description you hear, write the letter in the box that corresponds to the order in which the events occurred. Four pictures do not fit. You will hear the recording twice.

Well, I could see the accident very clearly from where I was because, as you know, the hotel overlooks the roundabout so I was looking down from the twentieth floor. I was standing on the balcony, so you could say I got a bird's eye view. What happened was that two cars were approaching the roundabout from the north one behind the other, almost about to enter it and there was a van already on the roundabout, going round it. The first car just drove straight on to the roundabout without stopping first and the van struck it twice. The first time the front of the van struck the front side of the car and then the van struck the car on the side again, at the back. Both vehicles continued moving and left the roundabout by the same exit, straightahead. Then just after they had left the roundabout they pulled over and stopped at the side of the road, the car in front and the van right behind it. By this time, the second car, which had stopped at the entrance to the roundabout, had come along and it stopped too, so there were three cars one behind the other, and all three drivers got out and looked at the damage. Then the third driver, the one who hadn't been involved in the accident, drove off, leaving the other two there.

SECTION B

You will hear an astronomer talking about the planet Mars. For questions 7–14, complete the table with the missing information. For each answer you will have to write down a number. Listen very carefully because you will hear the recording only once.

RADIO PRESENTER: … and for today's two-minute science spot, we have Bernard Smith, editor of 'Astronomy Today' who's going to talk to us about the planet Mars, which, as he's going to tell us, is clearly visible in the night sky at the moment.

BERNARD SMITH: That's right, Anna, you can see it with the naked eye and even with an ordinary pair of binoculars you can get a very good view. Now a lot of people think that Mars is like Earth but that's only true in the sense that the other planets are nothing like Earth at all. In fact there are many differences between Mars and Earth. The most obvious difference is that it is only about half the size. Whereas Earth has a diameter of 12,714 kilometres, the diameter of Mars is only 6,786 kilometres. Consequently, the force of gravity is much less on Mars. You could probably jump over a fence six metres high on Mars because it has only 38 per cent of Earth's gravity. Because Mars

52

is further from the sun than Earth – it's 141 million miles away compared with 93 million miles for Earth – it receives less than half the sunlight that Earth receives, only 43 per cent, to be precise. Obviously, because it is further away, it takes longer to go round the sun, almost twice as long, so a Martian year lasts 687 Earth days. The number of days in a Martian year is almost the same in Martian days because one thing which is almost identical on Mars and Earth is the length of the day. A Martian day is just slightly longer – 24 hours 37 minutes. One very obvious difference is that here on Earth when you look at the night sky you see one moon, whereas on Mars there are two, and they are called Phobos and Demos. As you probably know it is not possible to breathe the atmosphere on Mars because it is almost entirely carbon dioxide with only a very tiny amount of oxygen, a mere 0.1 per cent. However, if you were able to stand on the surface of Mars you would notice that some of its physical features, such as valleys and mountains are much bigger than anything on Earth. Our highest mountain is Mount Everest, which is 8,884 metres high, but there is a volcano on Mars which is three times higher at 26,000 metres.

SECTION C

You will hear a radio programme in which two people, Marcia and Robert, talk about the differences between electronic book discs and conventional printed books. During the interview they express various views. For questions 15–22, indicate which views are expressed by Marcia and which are expressed by Robert, by writing M for Marcia or R for Robert in the box provided. You may write both initials in one box if both express the same view. You will hear the piece twice.

RADIO PRESENTER: You've probably noticed that you can't buy long-playing records anymore – they've all been replaced by CDs. Is the same thing going to happen to books? Will books disappear from our lives and be replaced by electronic discs. We invited Marcia Brown, a computer expert, and Robert Smith, a novelist, to discuss the issues.

MARCIA: In my view, books are the dinosaurs of the 20th century and are about to become extinct. I think that by early next century books will only be produced in tiny quantities, if at all. We will obtain all the information and entertainment we need by inserting CD-ROM discs into handheld computers and reading from the screen. In fact, we can do this now. People will prefer this because, for example, the entire Oxford English Dictionary, twenty volumes in book form, weighing 66 kilograms, can be placed on a disc which you can carry around in your pocket. Because discs are much lighter than books, people will find them more convenient.

ROBERT: Well, I think that you are overstating your case, Marcia, because although the Oxford English Dictionary can fit onto one disc, it can't be used with a handheld computer. It has to be used with the kind of computer you

TEST 4

have on your desk, which can't be carried around. In any case, it is much quicker to find the information in a book, to look up a word in a dictionary, for example, than to locate the information on a computer screen. And even a handheld computer is heavier than a paperback book, although I agree that the actual discs are lighter though they are useless without something to play them on.

MARCIA: Well, of course, handheld CD-ROM players are very new and there is still a long way to go and a lot of things to improve. For example, they use up batteries very rapidly and the image, especially in colour, is not of good quality but these are early days. We are in the same position as we were with books in the sixteenth century. I think you are forgetting how quickly new things catch on and improve.

ROBERT: I can see that certain types of book, especially reference books such as encyclopaedias, are very suitable for using in the form of electronic discs because you can have all the information available in your home or office without lots of space being taken up by large books. But this question of the quality of the image is a very important one. It's possible to call up a street plan on your screen, for example, and find that you can't read the street names because they are blurred. Until that is improved, people will still prefer to read print from a page.

MARCIA: That may be true now, and it is also true that we still have several different formats for disc books – and we need to reach agreement on one format – and that prices are still higher than for conventional books, but these are early days. We have to look ahead and imagine how much things will have improved in thirty years time – that's when there won't be any more bookshops in your town.

SECTION D

You will hear five short extracts in which different people talk about danger and risk in their lives. You will hear the series twice.

*In **Task one** Letters A–H list the different people. As you listen indicate who is speaking by completing the boxes numbered 23–27 with the appropriate letter.*

*In **Task two** Letters I–P list the reasons for taking part in dangerous activities given by the people speaking in the five extracts. As you listen, put them in order by completing the boxes numbered 28–32 with the appropriate letter.*

1
Of course, it is nowhere near as dangerous as it looks to the people watching. A lot of it is special effects and there are a lot of things you can't see because they are not in the shot. And everything is very well planned in advance to minimise danger. But there is some danger and there are accidents. The main attraction for me is that we are paid very well and don't work very often, although our careers are rather short.

2

People think it is dangerous but in fact if you look at the statistics it is much, much safer than driving a car. It's just that jumping out into the air needs more nerve than getting into a car. Once you've jumped out, there's nothing more you can do – you totally rely on your equipment. The sense of exhilaration is marvellous, I just can't get enough of it.

3

I've lived here all my life and I know the area well and if people get into trouble up there I feel that I ought to try and help them. I just can't sit at home watching telly knowing that there's someone up there with a broken leg or something. There's a team of us of course, and if we can't get to the people easily they can bring in the helicopter but sometimes the weather is so bad that that's not possible. Then we just have to carry people down. It can take hours sometimes.

4

When you go underground, you have to squeeze through some very narrow spaces and that's very difficult mentally. Sometimes you think that you are going to be stuck, you feel trapped and you start to panic. Sometimes it happens that people completely freak out – and then it is really bad. It's the confined space, you see, some people just can't handle it. But what I like, is feeling the panic, sometimes letting it almost take over and then overcoming it and carrying on.

5

Well, for me it's a job and although it's not particularly well-paid, it's not boring and predictable like a lot of other jobs. You don't know from one day to the next what you will be doing. There's a lot of different things going on and you need to have a lot of different skills. When you hear the bell and jump into the appliance, and race through the streets, you never know what you're going to find when you arrive. Could be really dangerous, could be a simple job, you just don't know.

PAPER 5 SPEAKING (15 minutes)

PHASE A

(See p.25–26)

PHASE B1 (approximately 2 minutes)

THE ROBBERY (complete the story)

Candidate A is given the first and third (final) line drawings of a cartoon story about a robbery (p.117). One picture is missing, showing the middle of the story.

TEST 4

Candidate A is asked to describe the drawings and to try and imagine what might be shown in the missing picture (approximately one minute).

Candidate B is given the missing picture (p.49) and is asked to listen carefully to what Candidate A says so that at the end of the minute, he/she will be able to comment on how far Candidate A's description of the missing drawing is correct (approximately twenty seconds).

Then the candidates check the pictures together.

PHASE B2 (approximately 2 minutes)

JOBS (describe, hypothesise and comment)

Each candidate has the chance to talk for one minute about a photograph that each of them is given showing a person engaged in a particular profession (p.124 and p.128). Each candidate should say as much as they can about what the person is doing in the phoptograph and what the advantages and disadvantages of that particular job are.

When each candidate has described the picture, they comment on how far they agree/disagree with what the other has said, and indicate which job is better.

PHASE C (3 or 4 minutes)

PEDESTRIANISING THE HIGH STREET (evaluate, select and discuss)

Candidate A and B will be shown a town plan (p.95) and told that the local council is planning to prohibit cars from the shopping area. This will mean that traffic will have to be re-routed. Candidates should study the plan and suggest the ways in which they think the traffic should be re-directed.

PHASE D (3 or 4 minutes)

The examiners will now participate in the discussion and ask both candidates to comment further on the material from Phase C and then bring the interview to a close.

Test 5

ANSWER KEY

PAPER 1 READING

FIRST TEXT

1 B 2 E 3 A 4 B 5 C or D 6 D or C 7 F 8 D 9 A 10 C 11 D 12 E
13 F 14 B or C or D 15 D or B or C 16 C or D or B 17 B 18 D 19 B 20 E

SECOND TEXT

21 A 22 C 23 B 24 B 25 B

THIRD TEXT

26 D 27 F 28 A 29 E 30 B

FOURTH TEXT

31 C 32 A or B 33 B or A 34 C or D 35 D or C 36 E 37 G 38 A 39 F
40 F or G 41 G or F

PAPER 2 WRITING

Notes for guidance

SECTION A

1a This is a formal letter (Dear Mr Hughes + Yours sincerely). You have to inform Mr Hughes that three people will not be coming. You should, as tactfully as possible request a refund, perhaps just a partial refund or a refund if other guests book the rooms.

b This is an informal letter but must be serious in tone. You must either decide to make an exception and refund the money or explain as tactfully as possible that the money cannot be refunded unless the hotel agrees to refund it. You should make a sympathetic reference to the sad news that Tom and Sarah have received.

TEST 5

c This is an informal letter. There seems to be no reason to offer a refund unless Martin can provide good reasons for not wanting to go on the trip.

SECTION B

2 This is a semi-formal piece of writing. You may use headings if you wish but do not begin in the style of a report or a letter. There is no need to sign it but you can identify the type of visitor that you are, e.g. if you complain about the absence of guide-books in your language.

3 This is an informal letter. You should express your views in general terms without mentioning specific countries. Remember that for you the country where your friend lives is abroad. Mention the things that everyone benefits from in their own country – being near family and friends, familiar food and drink, and so on. Also mention the negative aspects of living abroad.

4 This is an article and needs a headline and sub-headings.

5 This is also an article and needs a headline and subheadings.

PAPER 3 ENGLISH IN USE

SECTION A

1 1 C 2 D 3 D 4 B 5 C 6 D 7 A 8 C 9 A 10 C 11 C 12 A 13 B
14 D 15 D

2 16 have 17 than 18 were 19 as 20 which/who 21 it 22 had 23 most
24 Until/Before 25 but 26 in 27 it 28 without 29 else 20 all

SECTION B

3 31 themselves 32 they 33 ✔ 34 ✔ 35 possibly 36 for 37 it 38 been
39 by 40 ✔ 41 are 42 a 43 has 44 least 45 such

4 46 goes back 47 about half 48 dates from 49 no need
50 excellent condition 51 nearly/almost/about 52 The possibility
53 plenty of 54 land 55 facilities 56 keep fit 57 well-protected/protected
58 road/rail 59 rail/road 60 negotiation

SECTION C

5 61 B 62 G 63 C 64 E 65 A

TEST 5

6 (Model answers)

66 In 1895, while teaching at the Sorbonne University in Paris he met and married Marie Sklodowska, a Polish student.

67 In 1898 they discovered two new radioactive elements and in 1903 they were awarded the Nobel prize for Physics, which they shared with Henri Becquerel, another scientist working in the same field.

68 The Curies' laboratory was very basic because they had little money to finance their research, which was both time-consuming and physically exhausting.

69 Pierre Curie was killed in a road accident in 1906 but Marie continued their work and succeeded in isolating pure radium in 1910, for which she was awarded a second Nobel prize, for chemistry, in 1911.

70 The discoveries made by the Curies were of great importance because they made it possible to treat many diseases which had previously been untreatable.

71 Marie Curie made no money from her discoveries because she refused to patent them, which meant that medical products based on them could be manufactured by anyone, anywhere, without the permission of or payment to the discoverer.

72 Marie Curie died in 1934, probably because of the effects of working with radioactive material for many years with no protection from its dangers.

PAPER 4 LISTENING

SECTION A

1 ✓ **2** ✓ **3** X **4** ✓ **5** ✓ **6** ✓ **7** ✓ **8** X

SECTION B

9 11.30 am **10** Lecture Room B **11** 308 **12** 7.15

13 room key
14 refund   } (in any order)
15 social programme

SECTION C

16 age **17** 45 **18** overweight/over 65 **19** good as before **20** pace/speed
21 body/weight **22** slim/lose weight **23** four hours **24** immediately after
25 ill/slightly ill/under the weather

TEST 5

SECTION D

Task one
26 E   27 H   28 C   29 G   30 B

Task two
31 L   32 K   33 P   34 O   35 M

TAPESCRIPT

SECTION A

You will hear a short talk about 'Safety in the Home'. Some of the pictures below illustrate dangers mentioned by the speaker and some do not. Put a tick in the box next to the picture, if the speaker mentions that point. Put a cross in the box if the picture illustrates a point not made by the speaker. You will hear the recording twice.

PRESENTER: In the second of our series on 'Safety in the Home', Amanda Brown talks about how to protect small children from danger.

AMANDA BROWN: It may seem an obvious point but you should always remember that small children are, well, small and are therefore looking up at things which we grown ups are looking down at. This means that children often can't see what is on a table. A child who pulls at the hanging flex of an iron probably can't see the iron, so be particularly careful about the use of irons. They're hot as well as heavy. For the same reason, always turn the handles of saucepans inwards when they are on the cooker. Don't leave them sticking out. Small children can grab them and cause hot liquid to fall down on them. As well as pulling at things, small children like to run about a lot, so if you have internal glass doors in your house make sure they are fitted with safety glass. If they are not, you can cover them with plastic safety film. Don't leave bottles of bleach, disinfectant or other cleaning products on the floor where children can find them. Lock them up or keep them out of reach. Another danger is doors opening and closing. Always open doors slowly and carefully, checking if a child is behind the door and don't let children put their fingers in the doorframe – this is really dangerous. If you see children doing this, warn them not to. Because children like to put their fingers in dangerous places, it is advisable to fit plastic covers to electricity sockets. This stops small fingers from going in and also prevents children from plugging in electrical devices by themselves and possibly causing fires or injuring themselves in some way. If you use the socket, remember to put the cover back in.

TEST 5

SECTION B

You will hear a message on your telephone anwering machine about important changes to the timetable of a conference that you are going to attend in a few days' time. For questions 9–15 make a note of the new details. Listen very carefully because you will hear the recording only once.

This is Elizabeth Jenkins, conference secretary. I'm ringing you because we have had to make some last minute changes that affect you and there isn't time to write to you before the start of the conference. For reasons that I won't go into now, we have had to shorten the conference by half a day and this has had a knock-on effect on various activities. As far as you are concerned it means that your talk is now on Saturday at 11.30 a.m. and not 2.30 p.m. as you were previously advised. It is still timed to last an hour so you will finish just in time for lunch, which begins at 12.30. We hope that this does not cause you too much inconvenience, and we apologise. The place of the talk is still the Science Block, but it is in Lecture Room B not D and you will need to ask the porter to open it for you as it is normally kept locked. Room B has the video equipment that you requested and room D doesn't. The room in which you will be staying has also been changed, I'm afraid. It's now room 308 in the Rochester Building. You can pick up the room key from reception when you arrive. Just tell the receptionist the number – 308 – and she'll give you the key. The time of the Wine Reception has also been changed. It will now start at 7.15 and last for about an hour, finishing just before dinner at 8.15. When you arrive, remember to pick up a refund from reception. We have to make a small refund because the conference is half a day shorter than planned. The receptionist will also give you a revised social programme, although fortunately changes to the social programme have been very small.

SECTION C

You will hear a radio interview with a doctor, about health and sport. For questions 16–25, complete the notes using one to three words or numbers. You will hear the piece twice.

INTERVIEWER: Dr David Green, who specialises in sports medicine, has joined us in the studio today and has some advice for people who are thinking of taking up a sport. Dr Green, what factors do we have to consider if we are thinking of taking up a sport?

DR GREEN: Well, the first thing to consider is your age. Up to about the age of forty-five, you can take up any sport providing that you have no particular medical problems. If you are carrying a few extra kilos, or if you smoke, you should avoid such sports as squash, fencing and judo. By the age of sixty-five, even healthy people should avoid those sports.

INTERVIEWER: Why is that?

DR GREEN: Because such sports involve sudden bursts of energy which are not completely under your control. You have to respond to what your opponent does or to what the ball is doing. There can be rapid and sudden increases in the heartbeat, and this can cause problems for some people.

INTERVIEWER: But what if people have been practising these sports all their lives?

DR GREEN: Ah, well, that's a different matter. If people have been practising sports regularly they can probably continue for many years. We're talking about taking up sports for the first time. One danger, however, is that people who practised sport when they were young, don't do it for a few years and then take it up again, expect to be as good as they were before. In fact, such people should start again from the beginning.

INTERVIEWER: Are there any sports which are generally safe and suitable for everyone, even people who are older or not in the best of health?

DR GREEN: Well, probably the safest of all is walking, fairly vigorous walking that is, which is safe for everyone. But sports such as swimming and cycling are a good choice because you can control your own pace, go as slowly or as fast as you wish. And the body is supported by the water or by the saddle, so you don't get the problems caused by repeated impact of the foot on the ground, which you do get with running. But even when people have chosen the right sport for their age, level and health, they often go about things in the wrong way.

INTERVIEWER: Can you give some examples of that?

DR GREEN: Well, people often think that exercise will get rid of excess fat but it won't, unless it is combined with a calorie-controlled diet as well. It takes hours and hours of exercise to burn up tiny amounts of fat – you would have to run for four hours just to burn up 100 grams of fat, for example. Another misconception is to do with cooling down after exercise. Most people understand the importance of warming up before you start, if you don't do that you risk tearing muscles and ligaments, but when they finish exercising many people go straight into a cold shower, or even worse, straight into the sauna, which is a very bad thing to do. It is vital to cool down before doing those things because sudden changes in temperature are not good for you, in fact they can be very dangerous. The worst thing of all, in my opinion, is for people to continue exercising when they have a cold or some minor infection. There have been more than a few cases of professional sportsmen dying because they have continued training while they were ill. So if you are feeling under the weather, stop your exercise programme until you have fully recovered.

TEST 5

SECTION D

You will hear five short extracts in which different people talk about accidents that they have had. You will hear the series twice.

*In **Task one** Letters A–H list the types of accident. As you listen, indicate what is being described by completing the boxes numbered 25–29 with the appropriate letter.*

*In **Task two** Letters I–P list different feelings experienced immediatley after the accident by the people speaking in the five extracts. As you listen, put them in order by completing the boxes numbered 30–34 with the appropriate letter.*

1
Well, I couldn't believe it. I just looked up and there it was right in front of me. I mean, it shouldn't have been there. It'd just pulled out suddenly. I couldn't avoid it, and in those days nobody wore a helmet, I mean you see a lot of people wearing helmets now but years ago nobody did. Well, I almost stopped in time. The brakes were a lot better than I thought and I didn't hit it, although I fell off and cut my leg a bit. I couldn't believe it. I'd expected much worse.

2
Well, it was the first time I'd tried it and I wasn't very good at it and I wasn't really enjoying it either. It was the last day and I was practising and I saw this, well, I don't know what it was, a sort of depression, there was probably a small stream underneath. Anyway, it sort of went down, and I thought I could just sail across it, you know, through the air and onto the other side but of course I hit the opposite bank and broke my leg, quite badly, because the bindings didn't release as easily as they do now. I felt like a complete idiot. It was so unnecessary.

3
It was deliberate. It wasn't an accident at all. He saw how close I was to scoring and just decided to stop me. And nobody saw it, not even the referee. It really messed my knee up. I was off for the rest of the season.

4
Somehow I knew he wouldn't get over it – it was just too high for him but it was too late to stop him. I knew we would fall. I was just hoping I wouldn't get hurt too badly and I suppose a broken wrist isn't too bad. You have to accept the occasional accident. It's inevitable if you go out a lot. It hasn't put me off.

5
Well, I could feel it going over and knew I couldn't stop it. The thing was, I didn't expect to be rescued. I was hundreds of miles from anywhere in a really remote area and in those temperatures you can't last for more than a couple of hours, even with a lifejacket. I had no hope at all. I hate to admit it now but I

actually started crying, but obviously no one could hear. It was a miracle someone spotted me.

PAPER 5 SPEAKING

PHASE A

(See p.25–26)

PHASE B1 (approximately 2 minutes)

STREET SCENE (describe and hypothesise)

Candidate A is given a photograph of a street scene showing how the place looked 100 or so years ago (p.120). candidate B has a photograph that shows the same scene today (p.126).

Candidate A has one minute in which to describe the photograph to Candidate B as fully as possible, describing what the photograph shows and how they think things might have changed in the last hundred years.

Candidate B listens to Candidate A and at the end of one minute says how accurate Candidate A's assessment of the changes has been.

The candidates then look together at the photographs and compare them.

PHASE B2 (approximately 2 minutes)

HOUSES (put the photographs in the correct order)

Candidate B is given a sheet containing six photographs of houses (p.124) and is asked to describe them in one minute so that Candidate A can put them in the correct order.

Candidate A is given a sheet containing the same photos but printed in a different order.

At the end of one minute, Candidate A is asked in what order he/she thinks the photos were described (approximately twenty seconds).

The candidates then compare photographs.

PHASE C (3 or 4 minutes)

LEISURE ACTIVITIES (evaluate and select)

Candidate A and B are each given seven photographs of leisure activities (p.127).

Together they are asked to consider the most suitable activity for each of the following:

a ten-year old boy;

a mother and a young toddler;

an office worker who wants to do something during the lunch break;

a fit retired person of 65.

PHASE D (3 or 4 minutes)

The examiners will now participate in the discussion and ask both candidates to comment on the material from Phase C and then bring the interview to a close.

ANSWER SHEET FOR PAPER 1 READING

ANSWER SHEET FOR PAPER 3 ENGLISH IN USE
(This is the first sheet only)

ANSWER SHEET FOR PAPER 4 LISTENING